Write Through Scripture

A 90-Day Challenge to Read & Write

Through the Gospels

By Stacie Nelson

Copyright © 2016 by Stacie Nelson

Faithfully Nourished, LLC

Printed in the United States of America

First Printing, 2016

www.StacieNelson.com

Introduction

This *Write Through Scripture* journal idea began when a friend and I were discussing our desire to dig into the Word of God. We were both in busy seasons of life and needed some accountability and motivation.

I knew I didn't have time for hours of study and prayer each and every day, but I also knew it was absolutely critical to connect with God and read His Word. How could I best do that?

My thoughts turned to a time in my life when I not only read Scripture—I copied it, too. Writing down Scripture was transformative in my journey. It forced me to slow down and "chew" on the Word. It helped me notice details I had previously skipped, and it helped me memorize Scripture more easily.

That's when the idea for this journal was born. I knew I wanted to combine reading and writing the Word, and the Gospels seemed the perfect place to begin.

My prayer is this simple journal will be a way for you to grow in faith and to be challenged and changed by the Word of God.

Blessings,

Stacie Nelson

How to Use this Book

Write Through Scripture journals are designed to be minimalistic and extremely simple to use. This isn't an in-depth Bible study with daily readings or thoughts on the passage. Instead, this journal is designed to help you focus and feast on God's perfect Word. This particular journal will take you on a 90-day journey through the Gospels. There are no right or wrong ways to use it, but here are sample ideas for each section of the daily pages:

Read: Read the passage aloud or read it silently.

Write: Write the passage.

Think: Think about how the Scripture applies or what God is saying in this passage. Write down a few thoughts or draw/ sketch what you've learned.

Thank: Choose gratitude. Write one or more things you are thankful for in the box.

Pray: Jot down a prayer or prayer requests in the box.

Depending on how much time you have each day, you may also choose to utilize commentaries, dictionaries, and other Bible study tools if you would like to dig even deeper in the Word.

Let's begin!

Date:

Read: Matthew 1

Write: Matthew 1:21-23

Think

Thank

Pray

Date:

Read: Matthew 2

Write: Matthew 2:9-11

Think

Thank

Pray

Date:

Read: Matthew 3

Write: Matthew 3:16-17

Think

Thank

Pray

Date:

Read: Matthew 4

Write: Matthew 4:23-25

Think

Thank

Pray

Date:

Read: Matthew 5

Write: Matthew 5:3-10

Think

Thank

Pray

Date:

Read: Matthew 6

Write: Matthew 6:9-13

Think

Thank

Pray

Date:

Read: Matthew 7

Write: Matthew 7:7-11

Think

Thank

Pray

Date:

Read: Matthew 8

Write: Matthew 8:23-27

Think

Thank

Pray

Date:

Read: Matthew 9

Write: Matthew 9:35-38

Think

Thank

Pray

Date:

Read: Matthew 10

Write: Matthew 10:1-4

Think

Thank

Pray

Date:

Read: Matthew 11

Write: Matthew 11:28-30

Think

Thank

Pray

Date:

Read: Matthew 12

Write: Matthew 12:35-37

Think

Thank

Pray

Date: **Read:** Matthew 13

Write: Matthew 13:44-46

Think

Thank

Pray

Date:

Read: Matthew 14

Write: Matthew 14:16-20

Think

Thank

Pray

Date:

Read: Matthew 15

Write: Matthew 15:17-20

Think

Thank

Pray

Date:

Read: Matthew 16

Write: Matthew 16:24-27

Think

Thank

Pray

Date:

Read: Matthew 17

Write: Matthew 17:20-21

Think

Thank

Pray

Date:

Read: Matthew 18

Write: Matthew 18:15-17

Think

Thank

Pray

Date:

Read: Matthew 19

Write: Matthew 19:23-26

Think

Thank

Pray

Date:

Read: Matthew 20

Write: Matthew 20:25-28

Think

Thank

Pray

Date:

Read: Matthew 21

Write: Matthew 21:9-11

Think

Thank

Pray

Date:

Read: Matthew 22

Write: Matthew 22:36-40

Think

Thank

Pray

Date:

Read: Matthew 23

Write: Matthew 23:23-26

Think

Thank

Pray

Date:

Read: Matthew 24

Write: Matthew 24:42-44

Think

Thank

Pray

Date: **Read:** Matthew 25

Write: Matthew 25:35-36, 40

Think

Thank

Pray

Date:

Read: Matthew 26

Write: Matthew 26:26-29

Think

Thank

Pray

Date:

Read: Matthew 27

Write: Matthew 27:45-46, 50-51

Think

Thank

Pray

Date:

Read: Matthew 28

Write: Matthew 28:18-20

Think

Thank

Pray

Date:

Read: Mark 1

Write: Mark 1:2-5

Think

Thank

Pray

Date:

Read: Mark 2

Write: Mark 2:15-17

Think

Thank

Pray

Date:

Read: Mark 3

Write: Mark 3:3-5

Think

Thank

Pray

Date: **Read:** Mark 4

                              Write: Mark 4:15-20

Think

Thank

Pray

Date: Read: Mark 5

                         Write: Mark 5:25-29

Think

Thank

Pray

Date:

Read: Mark 6

Write: Mark 6:1-6

Think

Thank

Pray

Date:

Read: Mark 7

Write: Mark 7:6-9

Think

Thank

Pray

Date:

Read: Mark 8

Write: Mark 8:27-29

Think

Thank

Pray

Date:

Read: Mark 9

Write: Mark 9:33-35

Think

Thank

Pray

Date:

Read: Mark 10

Write: Mark 10:13-16

Think

Thank

Pray

Date: **Read:** Mark 11

              Write: Mark 11:22-25

_____

_____

_____

_____

_____

_____

_____

_____

_____

_____

Think

Thank

Pray

Date:

Read: Mark 12

Write: Mark 12:41-43

Think

Thank

Pray

Date:

Read: Mark 13

Write: Mark 13:5-10

Think

Thank

Pray

Date:

Read: Mark 14

Write: Mark 14:32-36

Think

Thank

Pray

Date: **Read:** Mark 15

                          Write: Mark 15:22-26

Think

Thank

Pray

Date:

Read: Mark 16

Write: Mark 16:1-6

Think

Thank

Pray

Date:

Read: Luke 1

Write: Luke 1:30-33

Think

Thank

Pray

Date:

Read: Luke 2

Write: Luke 2:8-12

Think

Thank

Pray

Date:

Read: Luke 3

Write: Luke 3:15-16

_____

_____

_____

_____

_____

_____

_____

_____

_____

_____

_____

Think

Thank

Pray

Date:

Read: Luke 4

Write: Luke 4:17-19

Think

Thank

Pray

Date: **Read:** Luke 5

Write: Luke 5:22-25

_____

_____

_____

_____

_____

_____

_____

_____

_____

_____

_____

_____

Think

Thank

Pray

Date:

Read: Luke 6

Write: Luke 6:27-31

Think

Thank

Pray

Date:

Read: Luke 7

Write: Luke 7:44-47

Think

Thank

Pray

Date:

Read: Luke 8

Write: Luke 8:22-25

Think

Thank

Pray

Date:

Read: Luke 9

Write: Luke 9:1-6

Think

Thank

Pray

Date: **Read:** Luke 10

              Write: Luke 10:38-42

_____

_____

_____

_____

_____

_____

_____

_____

_____

_____

Think

Thank

Pray

Date:

Read: Luke 11

Write: Luke 11:33-36

Think

Thank

Pray

Date:

Read: Luke 12

Write: Luke 12:22-26

Think

Thank

Pray

Date:

Read: Luke 13

Write: Luke 13:10-13

Think

Thank

Pray

Date:

Read: Luke 14

Write: Luke 14:12-14

Think

Thank

Pray

Date:

Read: Luke 15

Write: Luke 15:3-7

Think

Thank

Pray

Date:

Read: Luke 16

Write: Luke 16:10-13

Think

Thank

Pray

Date:　　　　　　　　**Read:** Luke 17

　　　　　　　Write: Luke 17:12-17

Think

Thank

Pray

Date:

Read: Luke 18

Write: Luke 18:1-8

Think

Thank

Pray

Date:

Read: Luke 19

Write: Luke 19:5-10

Think

Thank

Pray

Date:

Read: Luke 20

Write: Luke 20:21-25

Think

Thank

Pray

Date:

Read: Luke 21

Write: Luke 21:27-28

Think

Thank

Pray

Date:

Read: Luke 22

Write: Luke 22:67-70

Think

Thank

Pray

Date:　　　　　　　　**Read:** Luke 23

Write: Luke 23:39-43

Think

Thank

Pray

Date:

Read: Luke 24

Write: Luke 24:45-49

Think

Thank

Pray

Date:

Read: John 1

Write: John 1:1-5

Think

Thank

Pray

Date: **Read:** John 2

Write: John 2:18-22

_____

_____

_____

_____

_____

_____

_____

_____

_____

_____

_____

_____

_____

_____

Think

Thank

Pray

Date:

Read: John 3

Write: John 3:16-18

Think

Thank

Pray

Date: **Read:** John 4

             Write: John 4:11-14

Think

Thank

Pray

Date:

Read: John 5

Write: John 5:6-9

Think

Thank

Pray

Date:

Read: John 6

Write: John 6:32-35

Think

Thank

Pray

Date:

Read: John 7

Write: John 7:37-41

Think

Thank

Pray

Date:　　　　　　　　　　**Read:**　John 8

　　　　　　　　　　Write:　John 8:7-11

Think

Thank

Pray

Date:

Write: John 9:1-7

Think

Thank

Pray

Date:

Read: John 10

Write: John 10:7-11

Think

Thank

Pray

Date:

Read: John 11

Write: John 11:21-26

Think

Thank

Pray

Date:

Read: John 12

Write: John 12:44-46

Think

Thank

Pray

Date:

Read: John 13

Write: John 13:12-16

Think

Thank

Pray

Date:

Read: John 14

Write: John 14:1-4

Think

Thank

Pray

Date:

Read: John 15

Write: John 15:12-17

_____

_____

_____

_____

_____

_____

_____

_____

_____

_____

_____

_____

_____

Think

Thank

Pray

Date: **Read:** John 16

Write: John 16:7-11

Think

Thank

Pray

Date:

Read: John 17

Write: John 17:15-17

Think

Thank

Pray

Date:

Read: John 18

Write: John 18:36-37

Think

Thank

Pray

Date:

Read: John 19

Write: John 19:33-37

Think

Thank

Pray

Date:

Read: John 20

Write: John 20:26-29

Think

Thank

Pray

Date:

Read: John 21

Write: John 21:15-17

Think

Thank

Pray

Date:

Read: Acts 1:1-11

Write: Acts 1:1-3

Think

Thank

Pray

Thank you joining me on this journey!

Learn more about the 90-day challenge,

find other resources I've written,

or connect with me at

www.StacieNelson.com

Made in the USA
Middletown, DE
24 September 2017